"The book, *Empowering Teens To Build* really helped me when I was at a low point. It helped me get back on track with my thinking and gave me more power and energy. After reading this book, I felt more positive and happy."

   -Adam Loewenheim, age 15

"This book contains everything that I have ever felt. It helped me to better understand myself and to make positive changes in my life. I didn't realize that I was coming from low self-esteem when I put other people down to make myself feel better. I think everyone should read the dating tips section. I agree with the idea that most people confuse codependence with love. These tips will help me look at things in the future more carefully."

   -Amy Davison, age 16

"*Empowering Teens To Build Self-Esteem* gave me a grasp of how to deal with my family better. I read it at the time my parents were going through a divorce. I also learned to think about myself and my feelings when I am in a new relationship with a guy. It is not a good idea to depend totally on a guy for everything. This book made me think about being more independent and not to get too attached too soon."

   -Jamie Rinkoff, age 16

"This book taught me what I did not know about myself. I learned that I'm going to be okay no matter what, that no one can take away what you have inside of you. I also learned there are different parts of me inside that have different feelings. I recommend this book to other teen-agers because it explains things we were never taught. It takes over where everyone else leaves off."

   -Christine Snitzer, age 18

This is a very good book about believing in yourself. It changes the way you think about things. It makes you think about what you are doing before you do them. I learned that mistakes can not ruin my life and that only I can make changes when I make a mistake. I learned also, that setting goals and achieving them can build self-esteem."

   -Travis Starnes, age 12

"*Empowering Teens To Build Self-Esteem* is packed with great advice, insight, wisdom and love.

Suzanne Harrill understands that most teenagers fear being judged and not fitting in...that they need at least one person in their lives who accepts them for the way they are. This book teaches them empowerment...to become their own best friend and to love and support themselves. More than that, Suzanne teaches them with awareness so they can change the things that can be changed.

Ms. Harrill speaks *to* your teenager...not *down* to your teenager. She guides them to understanding and betterment by teaching them the eight principals of self-esteem and how to build good feelings. She even provides tips for successful (and healthy) dating."
　　-Richard Fuller

"Suzanne's book, *Empowering Teens To Build Self-Esteem* supports adolescents in becoming more self-aware and responsible for their lives. Her book offers valuable information and processes that can help teenagers on their path to personal growth."
　　-Ester Wright, *Educational Consultant and*
　　　Author of "Good Morning Class - I Love You!"

"With your *Empowering Teens to Build Self-Esteem* book, you have really hit the target in helping others (especially youth) become aware of what high and low self-esteem is, and the power they have in doing something about it".
　　-J. D. Hawkins
　　　President, Preferred Learning
　　　Illinois State University - Faculty
　　　Executive Board Member - National Association for Self-Esteem

Empowering
Teens to Build
Self-Esteem

Suzanne E. Harrill, M. Ed.

Innerworks Publishing

Cover Design by Lightbourne Images
1-800-697-9833

Acorn Logo Design by Utopian Art
713/662-0561

Published by Innerworks Publishing
167 Glengarry Place
Castle Rock, CO 80108

ISBN:1-883648-04-1
ISBN:978-1-883648-04-6
Original ISBN: 1-883648-00-9

TABLE OF CONTENTS

Part V - More Information

Part VI - Dating Tips for Teens

Final Affirmation

This book is dedicated to my three daughters:
Lindy, Janna, and Sarah.

I thank the following people for helping create this book:
Diane Langley, Sheila Kruse O'Neil
and Susan Thomas Jerke.

The star graphics were originally created by Diane
Wilkinson. They were adapted from the Children's Self-
Esteem Cards and the book I am a Star,
both by this author.

The theme, or idea, of this book is:

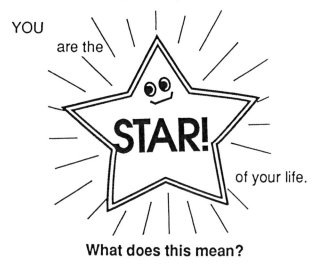

YOU are the **STAR!** of your life.

What does this mean?

It means:

- ★ You are in charge of the thoughts in your mind.
- ★ You are in charge of the things that you say.
- ★ You are in charge of the things that you do and how you do them.

Only YOU live inside your body.

You are the main character of your life script. You are also in charge of directing and writing this script, as well as editing, rewriting, recasting characters, and redoing scenes you do not like. As you take this job of being YOU seriously, you empower yourself to create a life that you want to live and will enjoy.

PART I

GETTING
STARTED

INTRODUCTION:

Hi! My name is Suzanne Harrill and I am excited about sharing with you information that may change your life. My experience has shown me that most teens do not like to look at themselves because they are afraid they will not like what they see. And I am talking about more than physical appearance. If they did take a look, however, they could get beyond judging what they see, and on with self-empowerment. This would positively influence the quality of their life.

"HOW DO I DO THAT?" YOU MIGHT BE ASKING.

1. First, you would learn that most other teens have similar inner problems, with thoughts and feelings of self-doubt, criticalness, and wanting to be accepted. This is covered up with a public face or mask for friends to see, which hides many feelings of insecurity. Most teens, in fact, will admit, if you talk to them privately, that they suffer from a lack of confidence, a fear of being judged and not fitting in.

**SO YOU CAN SEE,
YOUR FEELINGS ARE PRETTY NORMAL...**

2. Second, you would learn there are specific things you need to know about yourself that would help ease you through those tough times, such as, discovering what your inner needs are.

For example, two common needs which many teens have are:

1. The need for at least one other person to talk to who accepts you the way you are without judging you.

2. The need to have the social skills and confidence to start a conversation with the opposite sex.

Believe it or not, once you get a clear understanding of your needs, you can begin learning ways to get those needs met. You might, for example, read about the information you need or you might talk to an older person whom you trust (teacher, counselor, minister) or you might take a positive risk.

Examples of positive risks are to make eye contact and smile at someone you would like to get to know, or saying "hi" first to someone you do not know.

GETTING YOUR NEEDS MET
IS VERY IMPORTANT...

3.   Third, you would become your own best friend. This book will be about teaching you just that. There are actual things you can do to love and support yourself.

Yes, it is okay to love yourself and no, that is not going to make you an egotistical, obnoxious (self-centered) person. To let you in on a little secret, those irritating know-it-alls, who dominate and push themselves on others are really suffering from low self-esteem. In fact, a person with either an inferiority complex or a superiority complex has a self-esteem problem.

High self-esteem is a balanced place of quietly knowing you are okay. It is not telling others how smart or how popular you are or you aren't.

LOVING YOURSELF BEGINS BY BEING YOUR OWN BEST FRIEND...

4.   Fourth, you would learn to solve your own particular problems. Most people are not aware of the fact that they can make choices to think and act differently in order to have positive experiences in life.

No one wants to feel like a victim of circumstance; yet, many teenagers report feeling powerless over their lives. Teens need to learn to distinguish between what must be accepted in life, such as, hair, eye, or skin color, and what can be changed, such as, grades, relationships, or degree of physical fitness.

**YOU CAN EMPOWER YOURSELF TODAY BY
CHANGING THE THINGS THAT
CAN BE CHANGED --
THAT IS, ONCE YOU ARE AWARE OF THEM.**

5. Another way to build your self-esteem is to keep a journal of your thoughts and feelings, reactions to people, events, and insights. It is important to list your needs, wants, and goals as you become aware of them. Then, if you forget these things, you can review your journal, gaining insights and information when you need them again.

Buy a notebook today to use as your journal. Remember this is not English class, so no one will look for misspelled words. This is only for you.

A list of journal questions is on page 61.

JOURNAL WRITING HELPS YOU
GET TO KNOW YOURSELF...

6. Finally, developing and evaluating your goals is an important part of feeling good about yourself. If you do not think about and see in your mind possible outcomes to events, and possible interactions with others, they probably will not happen. So goals, even if you change them often, are very important to give you some structure and direction in life. Without goals, you will bounce around life like a cork floating in the ocean. Other peoples' goals and pictures will replace yours.

Take the time right now to write down some of your goals. Under each goal, list at least three steps you might take to accomplish each goal.

EXAMPLE: I want to be healthier.

        a. Eat dessert only once a week.

        b. Walk 1/2 hour a day.

        c. Go to bed by 10:00 P.M.

**GOALS EMPOWER YOU
BY GIVING YOU DIRECTION...**

GETTING TO KNOW YOURSELF

It is important to get to know yourself in order to build self-esteem. One way to get started is to take the Self-Esteem Awareness Indicator for Teens on page 10. It will start you thinking. At the the end of the book on page 68 is a Self-Esteem Awareness Indicator for your parents and on page 67 one for younger children, in case you might have younger brothers or sisters.

TEEN SELF-ESTEEM
AWARENESS INDICATOR

On the next page is a self-esteem indicator. This is NOT a test. In fact your answers are just for your personal use. By rating your answers, you will receive some feedback on areas where you might need help. It is helpful to use the Teen Self-Esteem Awareness Indicator in a discussion group with other teens. Maybe you could do this sometime.

Rate yourself on a scale of 0-4 for each question as to your current feelings and behaviors.

0 = I NEVER feel or behave that way.

1 = I RARELY feel or behave that way (25% of the time).

2 = I SOMETIMES feel or behave that way (50% of the time).

3 = I USUALLY feel or behave that way (75% of the time).

4 = I ALWAYS feel or behave that way (100% of the time).

TEEN SELF-ESTEEM AWARENESS INDICATOR

_____ 1. My feelings about myself are dependent on other people's opinions.

_____ 2. I get my feelings hurt easily.

_____ 3. I find it difficult to be myself when someone popular is near me.

_____ 4. I am uncomfortable if my friends know that I make good grades or am proud of my achievements.

_____ 5. I find it difficult to say no when my friends want to do something of which adults would not approve.

_____ 6. I do not like to be alone.

_____ 7. I see people's faults before I see their good points.

_____ 8. I say positive, kind things to myself in my mind with my self-talk.

_____ 9. I feel my own feelings and think my own thoughts, even when those around me think or feel differently.

_____10. I am a good person, even when I make mistakes or behave badly.

_____11. I am of equal value to all other people. I am not "better than" or "less than" anyone else.

_____12. I forgive myself and others for making mistakes and being unaware.

_____13. I accept responsibility for my choices, both wise and unwise, and willingly accept the consequences.

_____14. I develop my interests and use my talents.

_____15. I choose to love and respect every human being, including myself.

This is not scored like a test. _A person with high self-esteem would score low on the first seven statements and high on the last eight. This indicator gives you a place to start thinking. It is not a measure of your worth, only an indicator of where you might need help._
Note to teachers: these make good discussion and journal questions.

PART II

SELF-ESTEEM
IN
GREATER
DETAIL

NOW LET US LOOK AT SELF-ESTEEM IN GREATER DETAIL.

WHAT IS SELF-ESTEEM?

Self-Esteem is how you feel about yourself. You consciously and unconsciously send thoughts and opinions about yourself to yourself. These thoughts can be accurate and helpful or they can be false and damaging. To build self-esteem, you need to consciously think and say positive, honest things to yourself in your mind.

WHAT IS HIGH SELF-ESTEEM?

High self-esteem is a feeling of total acceptance and love for yourself as you are. It is where you respect and value yourself as a worthwhile human being. It is honestly seeing your good and not-so-good points. And it is taking care of yourself so you can become what you are capable of being.

High self-esteem is:

★ Liking yourself.

★ Knowing yourself and only trying to be you.

★ Being kind to yourself and others.

★ Taking risks and learning new things.

★ Accepting yourself even if you want some parts of you changed.

★ Honestly assessing your strengths and weaknesses without excessive pride or shame.

★ Taking responsibility for your own life.

★ Admitting when you have a problem or make a mistake.

★ Making amends if you find you have hurt someone.

★ Developing your talents and interests.

★ Balancing activities and quiet time.

★ Learning from your mistakes.

★ Being willing to accept the consequences of your choices with regard to your thoughts, feelings, and behaviors.

★ Standing up for yourself.

★ Loving being you.

WHY DO PEOPLE HAVE LOW SELF-ESTEEM?

A few of the more common reasons people develop low self-esteem are:

★ Believing the negative and hurtful words and actions of others.

★ Living with people who did not or do not love and respect themselves.

★ Having negative thoughts about performance, looks, family income level, and I.Q., to name a few.

★ Being under- or over-protected as a child.

★ Not being taught, "I am good and of value and loved no matter what."

★ Doubting that you were loved by one or both parents. (The absence of a parent hurts, too.)

★ Being punished without ever being taught to separate "you" from your bad behavior.

★ Living in fear.

★ Being compared to others or to perfect standards that could not be met.

★ Being raised in a dysfunctional family.

★ Forgetting that you have a wise, intuitive inner voice.

★ Thinking "you" are your possessions, clothes, car, grades, job, or I.Q.

★ Not learning from mistakes.

How do I know if someone has low self-esteem?

That's easy. They will have some or all of the following characteristics of low self-esteem on pages 17 - 19. These are:

BEHAVIORS

THOUGHTS

FEELINGS

Some BEHAVIORS
of low self-esteem:

★ Hurting yourself in any way.

★ Being a bully or hurting others including your brothers, sisters, or parents.

★ Saying mean things to others.

★ Not keeping clean with your body or your clothes.

★ Not speaking up for yourself.

★ Talking too much or too little.

★ Needing to always be first or last.

★ Gossiping or making fun of others.

★ Breaking things or defacing property.

★ Taking things that do not belong to you.

★ Over or under eating.

★ Not trying new things because you might make a mistake.

Some THOUGHTS of low self-esteem:

★ Thinking that you are better than someone different from you.

★ Thinking others are better than you.

★ Thinking mean or negative things in your mind about yourself.

★ Thinking, "I don't count."

★ Thinking with "shoulds" or "oughts", which are value-judgements.

★ Secretly hoping someone will fail or hurt himself or herself.

★ Thinking only one way - your way - is right.

★ Forgetting to think about improving your life.

★ Pretending everything is OK when it's not.

★ Thinking you don't need anybody or any help.

★ Thinking you can't make it without a boyfriend or girl-friend.

Some FEELINGS of low self-esteem:

★ Feelings of hatred, resentment, or wanting to get even.

★ Feelings of jealousy and possessiveness.

★ Feeling wounded and hurt when others with low self-esteem put you down.

★ Many feelings of anger or sadness when you don't know why you are feeling angry or sad.

★ Being embarrassed and ashamed when you haven't done anything wrong.

★ Crying a lot.

★ Isolating yourself from others.

★ Feeling lonely much of the time.

Wow! You can see there are a lot of things to look for. Just remember that you might have only some of them. But, even if you have almost all of them, YOU can change the things you don't like.

PART III
IDEAS THAT BUILD POSITIVE SELF-ESTEEM

The Acorn Analogy
helps us understand
the Principles of Self-Esteem.

The acorn does the best it can do at each stage of growth along its life cycle to become a giant oak tree.

It can only grow to the degree that it has nurturing from nature: sunlight, rain water, and nutrients from the soil.

Even if the early start was less than perfect, the eager oak can accelerate its desire to grow at any time there are proper nutrients available.

You are like the acorn. You, too, are doing your best under the conditions in which you are growing. Add a little awareness and self-acceptance and watch you grow!!!

REMEMBER TO NURTURE YOURSELF.

WHAT ARE SOME IDEAS THAT BUILD POSITIVE SELF-ESTEEM?

The Eight Principles of Self-Esteem

1. *Accept Yourself Right Now...*

Accept yourself right now
just the way you are
with no strings attached.
That perfect time in the future
with the perfect you
does not exist.

You are okay
just the way you are,
even if you want to change
parts of yourself.

I'm OK!

**IT IS ALWAYS RIGHT NOW,
SO MY POWER IS IN LOVING MYSELF TODAY.**

2. *Look Inside Yourself, Not Outside Yourself, To Feel Good.*

"Out there" is dependent
*   on other people or*
other things to make
*   you feel good.*

"In here" (your thoughts,
*   beliefs, attitudes,*
and perceptions) is the
*   only thing over which*
you have complete control.

You must ultimately rely
*   on yourself, not the*
opinions or actions of others,
*   to feel good about yourself.*

I BUILD MY GOOD FEELINGS BY
REMEMBERING TO BE MY OWN BEST FRIEND.

3. Stop Value-Judging Yourself...

It is helpful to drop "shoulds"
     and "oughts" from your vocabulary.
They are a form of
     value-judging yourself.

It is irrevelant what you should
     do or should have done.
It is more important to ask yourself
     what you are or are not
     willing to do.

Then do it
     or forget it.

**BEING WILLING TO PAY THE
CONSEQUENCES OF MY CHOICES
BUILDS MY SELF-ESTEEM.**

4. Separate "You" From Your Behavior...

You are not your behavior.
You are the one who behaves.
You can dislike a behavior
without disliking yourself.

If you have a behavior that you
do not like in yourself,
know there is a reason for this
negative behavior.

When you discover your
hidden needs, you will
improve your choices
of behavior.

Journal writing
or talking to someone helps.

I AM GETTING TO KNOW MYSELF SO I CAN
WISELY CHOOSE MY BEHAVIOR.

5. *Stop Comparing Yourself To Others Or To A "Perfect" Standard...*

Your worthiness is what you were born with.

You lower your self-esteem if you

feel "better than" or "less than"

anyone else. You have only to be you.

Perfection is a goal, not a standard

to measure your worthiness.

Know you are learning and growing

with all the experiences in your life.

If you must compare,

do it only with yourself

to gauge your progress

and to set goals.

I AM INCOMPARABLE.

6. You Are Doing Your Best...

You can only do what you do
*   based on your level of awareness.*
If you want to change, you must gather
*   new information from teachers,*
self-help books, counselors, and observation
*   of others to expand your choices.*

There are many parts of you —
*   physical, emotional, mental, and spiritual.*
If you are dissatisfied in one area,
*   for example, intellectual performance,*
it may help to work on the emotional part of you
*   which in turn helps the mental.*
A positive change in any area
*   helps all of you.*

Forgive yourself for mistakes and
*   for taking time to change.*

I REMEMBER THE ACORN ANALOGY
TO HELP ME PRACTICE THIS IDEA.

7. *You Are Worthy Of Unconditional Love...*

Being worthy cannot be earned by your
accomplishments or your behaviors.
It is a gift to be accepted
by you from you.

You are worthy because you exist —
It is your birthright.

Love yourself unconditionally —
Even if no one else knows
how to do this for you.

I DESERVE LOVE AND RESPECT,
NO MATTER WHAT.

8. Take Responsibility For Your Life...

No one is to blame for the problems
    you are experiencing —
not you, not your parents,
    not your teachers, not your
    friends — no one.

Accepting responsibility begins the
    process of seeking a solution.
Only you have the power to solve
    your problems and live
    your life more fully.

You are the star of
    your life. Remember?!

I TAKE RESPONSIBILITY FOR MY LIFE NOW!

PART IV

BUILDING

GOOD

FEELINGS

How can you build good feelings about yourself?

Start by identifying and healing negative self-talk.

We all have a voice inside our minds that comments continually about everything we think, do, and say. This voice is critical and negative much of the time. To build self-esteem, it is necessary to change the negative, critical, self-talk to a kind, loving, and supportive voice inside our minds.

EXERCISE:

Begin by remembering the past week. What negative feeling memories do you have? Choose one. Go back in your mind and remember the things you said to yourself in your mind. For example, perhaps you were late to a job interview and your self-talk said, "You dummy, you didn't leave enough time, AGAIN! You are always late. You'll never get that job. You are so stupid. Nobody likes a late person."

This negative self-talk lowers your self-esteem. To change a negative habit such as being late, you need to break the cycle of inner abuse. Instead of beating yourself up in your mind, it is much more productive to build yourself up by saying kind, supportive, and problem-solving things to yourself.

A better way to talk to yourself would be, "I did not leave enough time. I will work on my issue with punctuality. My interview went well except for being late. I deserve this job. I have the skills and talents for this job."

Listen to your self-talk. Talk back to it and you will begin to feel better about yourself.

AFFIRMATIONS -
Good things to say to yourself

On the following pages are positive affirmations that build self-esteem. If you say the statements over and over, even out loud to yourself, you create positive self-talk in your mind, which eventually makes you feel good about yourself. After each affirmation is information to explain what the affirmation means. There is even room for you to write your own comments. Consider writing your own affirmations, perhaps on 3x5 cards.

Remember!

Say the statements over and over, out loud, until you feel the affirmation is true about YOU. You might even like to read the affirmations into a tape recorder and listen to your tape while you are relaxing or going to sleep at night.

See Positive Mind Pictures.

To empower yourself further, see positive pictures in your mind. If, for example, you want to feel confident giving a speech to your class, picture in your mind yourself breathing deeply, smiling, and feeling relaxed as you stand in front of the class. The more you can feel the mind picture,the more it helps you create the picture in real life. You build your good feelings by seeing and feeling positive mind pictures.

As you say the affirmations on the following pages, see and feel in your mind as if they are already true for you.

Let's Get Started!

I am the star of my life.

You are the main character of your own life, much as an actor in a play. You also write the script, direct, and edit your play. You can take responsibility for what you do, think, and say with your part when you know you are the star of your life.

I am responsible for my choices.

You are the one who thinks and makes choices for your life. When you take responsibility, you make choices that support yourself and others.

I am unique, one of a kind.

No two people are exactly alike. You feel good when you appreciate your special set of traits, abilities, and potentials. Life does not expect you to be anyone except yourself.

I am good, even when my behavior is bad.

No matter what the behavior, the inner essence of who you are is okay and good. You are not bad when your behavior is bad. Behavior is how you get your needs met. Many needs are unconscious.

I love and respect myself.

It is good to love yourself. You are worthy of dignity and respect. You will automatically treat other people with love and respect when you do this for yourself first.

I am like an acorn able to grow into the greater me.

We are all growing into our full-potential self, doing the best we can at each place along the journey of life. To grow, give yourself proper nutrients, such as, positive self-talk, exercise, nutrition, and a support system that you create for yourself.

I like myself.

It is important to be your own best friend. You have to live with yourself all the time. Why not get to like who you are? It makes life easier.

I stop:
* comparing myself to others.
* blaming myself.
* talking negatively to myself.

Bad habits lower self-esteem.

* It is a bad habit to get your self-worth from comparing yourself to others. You are okay whether you do better or worse than others.
* It is a bad habit to put yourself down for mistakes or bad behavior.
* It is a bad habit to put yourself down by saying mean things to yourself.

I laugh at myself sometimes.

It is best not to take yourself too seriously. Laughter heals. When you lighten up, you make wiser choices and you handle mistakes better. Laughter is a good way to express feelings of tension and discomfort, as well as joy and fun.

I feel kind and loving toward myself.

It is good to love yourself. Do not expect other people to love you — they may not know how. A person can only love you if they know how to love themselves.

I forgive others who have hurt me.

Many people don't know they have hurt your feelings. If they do things that sometimes hurt you, forgive them in your mind. This does not mean you have to stick around a bully and continue being hurt.

I am developing my talents and interests.

Expressing your talents and interests builds good feelings about yourself. They do not have to be talents that society values. They can be caring for animals or plants, developing a good mind, or playing a musical instrument. Time spent developing interests eliminates boredom and gives life meaning.

I, (YOUR NAME), **deserve**

- ★ to feel good.
- ★ to feel happy.
- ★ to feel confident.

It is okay to feel good, happy, and confident. These are components of high self-esteem. You begin by giving yourself permission to feel good, happy, and confident. It is never too late to grow these branches on your oak tree as you grow into your full-potential self.

I learn from all of my experiences, good as well as bad.

Everyday living is the school of life. We grow wiser every day by learning the lessons behind our experiences. Attention to these lessons will enable us to create a life with awareness — repeating what we like and stopping what we do not like.

I express my angry and hurt feelings and emotions by talking or writing in a journal.

It is a good idea to express negative emotions in a positive way. Denied emotions pop out when least expected in such things as being accident-prone, over-reacting, having many illnesses, or a lot of body pain. Hurting yourself or others is unacceptable and a symptom of low self-esteem. Discuss or write about negative emotions to encourage positive growth.

I accept all of my feelings. They are okay.

Feelings are not right or wrong. They are messages from your inner-self that are telling you something. You can use feelings as teachers to help you understand your thoughts and reactions to people and events in your life.

My body is my friend so I take care of it with proper sleep, exercise, and food.

A body is a very remarkable thing. Take care of it so it will last you a long time. It feels good to live in a healthy body.

I separate the inner me from my behavior.

The true you is inside you. This part of you is important to get to know. It has needs and wants. Sometimes you have behavior that is bad because you do not know yourself. When you know your inner-self, you make wiser choices so your behavior pleases you. You are not your behavior, you are the one who behaves.

I have the right to say "NO."

It is a good idea to always check in with your inner-self when friends want you to do things. The better you feel about yourself, the more you'll have the courage to risk rejection by saying "no" to things that are not good for you. By the way, it is usually a good idea to obey people in authority, such as, parents, teachers, or bosses.

I think about why I do things, so I can solve my problems.

The way out of your problems is to use your mind to think. As you study yourself, you can figure out why you do things. If you want to get different results, then you make different choices. This is how you learn.

I value myself.

It is a decision to value yourself. When this choice is made, you accept yourself totally, assets as well as imperfections. Your basic nature is good, no matter what your actions are.

I accept the way I look.

If you are critical of your looks, you need to determine what can be changed and what must be accepted. It keeps you feeling bad to focus on and be critical of what cannot be changed. You feel good when you learn to accept your looks.

I have the power to change many things I do not like in my life.

You have a mind, so you can think about solutions to your problems. It is up to you to take responsibility for finding solutions so that you like living your life.

I am of equal value to all other people.

No two people are alike and every single one is of equal value to all others. We are all part of the greater whole and the universe would not be complete without each of us. We have individual differences and potentials; yet we are all valuable.

I listen to my intuition. (My wise inner voice.)

You have a wise inner voice that can help you make good choices in your life. Sometimes it takes time to tell the difference between the wise voice and the negative, critical inner voice. Practice paying attention to your wise inner voice. Young people many times find this easier to do than adults.

I say kind things to myself.

Positive self-talk builds high self-esteem. When no one else is around, you have to live with yourself — so be a good friend to yourself and say good things to build your confidence and feelings of value.

I forgive myself when I make a mistake.

Everyone makes mistakes. Mistakes are how people learn and grow. They teach you to choose differently the next time the situation comes up again.

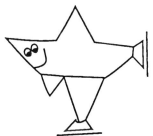

I am free to be me.

When you express your true self, it feels good. Get to know your inner-self, your needs, wishes, goals, values, and beliefs. Your true self is always good.

I take one day at a time.

When looking at problems, we sometimes get overwhelmed. It helps to slow down and just live today. Do what you need to do and can do today. Get the most out of today because yesterday is gone and tomorrow isn't here yet.

I am calm and peaceful.

You use your mind well when you are calm and peaceful emotionally. Remember, the messages you send your subconscious mind are what is expressed in your life.

I like to be alone sometimes.

It is healthy to know how to be alone and not be lonely. To always have people around and activities to do distracts you from your inner-self. There is great wisdom and creativity inside you that wants to come forward. It can do so only when you allow yourself time to be alone to listen.

I like to help others.

True giving, without an expectation of a return, results from a well-nourished self. When you take care of yourself and feel good about yourself, you can give unconditionally. Some people give because they are empty and need approval, acceptance, or love. It is wise to fill yourself up emotionally so your giving has no emotional "hooks" in it.

I make a difference.
My life counts.

We each have a special mission only we can fulfill. When you have your lower-level needs met — like food, safety, love — then you can contribute to the well-being of the place where you live — planet Earth — and the larger group — humanity. When you learn to value yourself, it is easy to make a difference by contributing to life.

I use my
time wisely.

We all have 24 hours in a day. It is wise to balance active or goal-oriented time with passive or non-directive time. You can be more balanced if you listen to your wise inner self each day to see if you need more or less activity.

I have friends who like me, support me, and respect me.

It is important to learn discrimination in your friendships. Not everyone is good for you. A good friendship is reciprocal (give and take). A good friend is one who helps you feel good being you.

I smile a lot.

Your outer expression shows how you are doing on the inside. As you grow in self-love and feelings of worthiness, it automatically shows on your face. Smiles open doors when you are relating to others.

I take positive risks.

To grow into your full-potential self, you need to expand your awareness. You do this by taking positive risks that teach you what is outside of your personal boundaries or universe. Sometimes you get fearful and do not want to take steps to solve problems. It took many tries to learn to walk when you were a toddler. Give that much effort to everything you try.

I set goals and have fun achieving them.

Over-achievers set goals so high that they never meet them, so they feel like a constant failure. Under-achievers also stay stuck with feelings of low self-worth because they are so fearful of failure or making a mistake that they never try. Set goals that are within reason of your capabilities. Goals are merely the direction you are going and can be fun and flexible.

I am strong and healthy.

The subconscious mind is non-thinking. The messages the conscious mind sends it are like programming a computer. Say positive things and your computer will do its best to do what you tell it. Say, "I am strong and healthy and my body wants to please me."

I know I am good.

All that is really important in sound self-esteem is that we know we are good and that our intentions are to do and be our best. This is an inner awareness not dependent on other people's opinions. Another way to say this is, "My inner spiritual essence is the real me."

Now that you've read all the way through the affirmations, go back and choose one statement that you did not feel was true about you at first. Repeat it again and again, until you really feel inside that it is true for you.

Do this with any affirmation you have a question about until all the affirmations feel true for you. You might want to share this book with a friend.

PART V

MORE

INFORMATION

JOURNAL THOUGHTS AND QUESTIONS

You do not have to answer these questions in order. Some you will come back to over and over during your whole life.

1. List your traits. Put an **L** next to the ones you like. Put a **D** next to the ones you do not like.

2. List your short term and long term goals. Put a time on these goals. What are the steps you need to take to get started meeting these goals? Are any of these goals unrealistic?

3. What is more developed in you -- your physical, emotional, mental, or spiritual self? Discuss what each one is and where you need help.

4. List your problems. Where did they start? Do you need outside help? If so, where can you go to get help?

5. Are you most like your mom or dad? Explain.

6. What do you find confusing or unpleasant about living in your family?

7. Who are you the closest to in life? Explain.

8. What do you want to change in yourself for self-improvement? Discuss.

9. List things you do to nurture yourself.

10. If you could improve one family relationship, which one would you choose? How would you begin?

11. Do you have self-discipline or does discipline need to come from outside yourself? Discuss.

12. List your needs. List your wants.

13. List what makes you feel you are loved.

14. What is your greatest fear? How do you handle your feelings? Do you need help from a counselor or from reading books?

15. What is the most negative thought you have about yourself? Change this to a positive affirmation.

16. Define what God means to you. Are you happy with your relationship with God? Discuss.

17. Take an event from your past -- one that still hurts or bothers you -- and write a letter to the person or people involved, expressing your feelings. Do not give them the letter. What did you learn from the person or experience?

18. Pretend you are writing a novel. As the author, choose the parents, family, and early life circumstances in order to create a context for the main character, you. Take your story up to the present time and explain your reasons for having these experiences, people, and events show up for your character. Now look into the future and show how this character can use those early life experiences to the best advantage. Where could the early experiences be a motivator to do or experience something down the road?
(Purpose: This exercise helps many people move beyond a difficult childhood, a traumatic event, or a difficult period in life.)

SUMMARY OF WAYS TO BUILD SELF-ESTEEM

1. **Say kind things to yourself.**

    Change negative self-talk to positive self-talk by saying positive affirmations such as:

    *   I am okay even when I make a mistake.

    *   I love and accept myself even if my mother, father, friend, or teacher does not show their love for and acceptance of me.

    *   I am good even when my behavior is bad.

2. **<u>Picture</u> what you want in your mind.**

    Change negative self-images to positive pictures, such as:

    *   See yourself standing tall, taking a deep breath as you preview in your mind a positive way to handle a challenging situation you must go through.

    *   See yourself studying to make a good grade.

3. **Make the 8 Keys of Self-Esteem part of your beliefs about yourself.**

    If you believe you must earn love and worthiness from sources outside yourself, you may need to change these false beliefs to:

    *   I am worthy simply because I am alive.

    *   I receive unconditional love from myself and do not expect this from others.

4.   Develop and share your talents.

- Take the word "talents" loosely. Talents do not have to be highly valued by society. It can be a talent of working with animals, plants, or senior citizens, to name a few.

- Get involved and help others.

- Pass on what you've learned.

5.   Create a support system.

- Join a support group.

- Take classes.

- Find a friend who is also working on building self-esteem.

- There is power in numbers, so have people around you who know and live these concepts.

6.   Keep a journal.

- Write your thoughts, feelings, and reactions to people and events.

- Write letters to people with whom you are angry; but, DO NOT give it to them.

7. Read other books.

Here are some to get you started. The library or a bookstore can order them if they do not have them.

- If You Don't Know Where You're Going, You'll Probably End Up Somewhere Else, by David Campbell, Ph.D., Argus Communications, Niles, Illinois 60648, 1974

- Take 10 To Grow, By Franklin D. Cordell, Ph.D. and Gale R. Giebler, Ph.D., Argus Communications, Niles, Illinois 60648, 1978

- Taking Charge of My Life: Choices, Changes & Me,by Ed Marmon and Marge Jarmin, The Barksdale Foundation, P.O. Box 187, Idyllwild, California 92549, 1988

- Teen Esteem, A Self-Direction Manual for Young Adults, by Dr. Pat Palmer with Melissa Alberti Froehner, San Luis Obispo, California 93406, 1989

- Why Am I Afraid To Tell You Who I Am? by John Joseph Powell, Argus Communications, Chicago, Illinois, 1969

The following books are available from Preferred Learning: 1-800-882-7734

- Feed Your Head: Some Excellent Stuff on Being Yourself, by Earl P. Hipp

- Fighting InvisibleTigers, A Stress Management Guide For Teens, by Earl P. Hipp

- Stick Up For Yourself, by Gushen Kaufman Ph.D. and Lev Raphael, Ph.D.

- S.E.E.K. (Self-Esteem Enhancement Kit) , by Stephanie Roth-Nelson

- TA For Teens, by Alvyn Freed, Ph.D.

SYMPTOMS OF HIGH SELF-ESTEEM

- Accepting yourself and others.

- Feeling joyful and loving.

- Allowing yourself to make mistakes, stumble and fall, and occasionally fail.

- Taking positive risks.

- Feeling capable of solving your problems.

- Losing fearful thoughts.

- Living in the NOW.

- Losing interest in value-judging and blaming (no "shoulds" and "oughts").

- Smiling frequently.

- Allowing people and circumstances to unfold.

- Accepting what must be by recognizing what you can and cannot change.

- Being balanced physically, emotionally, mentally, and spiritually.

CHILDREN'S SELF-ESTEEM AWARENESS INDICATOR

Here is a children's Self-Esteem Indicator if you have younger brothers or sisters.

Answer each question: T̲ for True, F̲ for False, or 0̲ for Maybe or Sometimes. Read to children who do not read yet and have them verbally answer.

_____ 1. I am good.

_____ 2. I love myself.

_____ 3. I have positive traits and negative traits and that is okay.

_____ 4. I am a valuable, worthwhile person.

_____ 5. I make a difference. My life matters.

_____ 6. I like myself the way I am, even if I want to change some parts of me.

_____ 7. I say positive, kind things to myself in my mind with my self-talk.

_____ 8. I like to be first and to win. I also can wait my turn and am a good loser.

_____ 9. I make mistakes sometimes and this is okay.

_____10. I am good even when my behavior is bad.

_____ Bonus Question: I am of equal value to all other people. I am not "better than" or "less than" anyone else even if my looks, talents, and traits are different.

Scoring: Give 10 points for all T answers, NO points for all 0 answers, and subtract 10 points for all F answers. This is not a test, simply an indicator. It gives feedback where a child needs help in building self-esteem. Discuss all statements that were not answered True. Children with low scores need help in building self-esteem.

THE ADULT SELF-ESTEEM
AWARENESS INDICATOR

On the next page is an adult Self-Esteem Indicator for older teens, parents, and teachers.

This is a tool to make you think and to help you become more aware of aspects affecting your self-esteem (love of self). It is not a test and is <u>not</u> to be used as a valid measurement of your self-worth.

Rate yourself on a scale of 0 to 4 as to your current feelings and behaviors.

> 0 = I NEVER feel or behave that way.
> 1 = I RARELY feel or behave that way (25% of the time).
> 2 = I SOMETIMES feel or behave that way (50% of the time).
> 3 = I USUALLY feel or behave that way (75% of the time).
> 4 = I ALWAYS feel or behave that way (100% of the time).

Score   Self-Esteem Statements

_____ 1. I accept myself the way I am right now. I like being who I am.

_____ 2. I am worthy, simply because I exist. I do not have to earn my worthiness.

_____ 3. I get my needs met before I meet the needs of others.

_____ 4. I do not let it get me down when other people blame or criticize me.

_____ 5. I always tell myself the truth about what I am feeling.

_____ 6. I do not compare myself to other people.

_____ 7. I feel of equal value to other people regardless of my performance, looks, I.Q., possessions, or achievements (or lack of them).

_____ 8. I take responsibility for my feelings and emotions. I do not blame others when I am upset, angry, or hurt.

_____ 9. I learn from my mistakes rather than use them to confirm my unworthiness.

_____ 10. I separate my behavior from my inner Self.

_____ 11. I understand that I can choose to love each human being without having an active relationship with them.

_____ 12. I accept other people as they are, even when they do not meet my expectations or I dislike their behaviors or beliefs.

_____ 13. I am not responsible for anyone else's actions, needs, thoughts, moods, or feelings, only for my own (exception...your children when they are young).

_____ 14. I feel my own feelings and think my own thoughts, even when those around me think or feel differently.

_____ 15. I am kind to myself and do not use "shoulds" and "oughts" to put myself down with value-judging comments.

_____ 16. I allow others to have their own interpretation and experience of me.

_____ 17. I look for something positive in each individual I meet.

_____ 18. I forgive myself and others for making mistakes and being unaware.

_____ 19. I accept responsibility for my interpretation of other people's behavior and my responses to them.

_____ 20. I do not dominate others or allow others to dominate me.

_____ 21. I am my own authority. I make decisions that are for my own and others' best interests.

_____ 22. I develop and use my talents.

_____ 23. I balance giving and receiving in my life. I have good boundaries with others.

_____ 24. I am responsible for changing what I do not like in my life.

_____ 25. I choose to love and respect every human being including myself.

Add up your score. There are a possible 100 points. Place no judgments on your score. Use the statements where you assigned a lower number as affirmations to build positive self-talk, perhaps writing them on 3x5 cards.

Examples and more information are given in the books <u>You Could Feel Good</u> and <u>Affirm Your Self Day By Day</u> by Suzanne E. Harrill, M.Ed., Innerworks Publishing.

PART VI

DATING TIPS FOR TEENS

SELF-ESTEEM AND DATING

Even though the emphasis of this book is learning how to love and respect yourself, it would not be complete without information to help you successfully relate to the opposite sex. Dating is usually of more interest than building self-esteem. However, if I can convince you that you really need high self-esteem to have a healthy, loving relationship, then you will read and reread this book until the information becomes a part of you.

To truly have a lasting love relationship with another it is important to understand and love yourself first. Awareness of self helps better prepare you for the journey of being in a loving relationship.

Most teens reverse the steps necessary to create a successful, intimate relationship. How do they do this? Many teens think the most important ingredient in creating an intimate relationship is finding someone to love them, rather than, first building a strong foundation of love and respect for themselves. Unhealthy love is learned from many of the adults in society by watching the themes in many movies, advertising in magazines, and on TV, as well as, dysfunctional relationships experienced in their own families.

For these reasons and more, many teens confuse romantic love with real love. Many also misinterpret codependence as love.

Romantic love is that intense feeling a person gets when there is a strong physical attraction in the beginning of a relationship. It is a very pleasant feeling. The purpose of this type of love is to get people together who might otherwise be too shy or fearful to get involved. Some people say romantic love has a biological purpose which is simply to insure our species will perpetuate itself. Try telling this to a person "in love" and they will not agree. Hopefully you are reading this at a time when you are receptive to what is being said.

Codependence is a state of losing yourself in a relationship. You place the other person's needs before your own. Over time you forget to take care of yourself and you even stop being yourself. Insecurity, dependency, control, and power struggles take over. It empowers you to learn to build security and control within by building your self-esteem. There are lots of books on the subject of codependency in case you are interested.

Intimacy, believe it or not, is the most successful between two people who know how to love and respect themselves first. High self-esteem is a must if you want to avoid the painful experiences of divorce in the future. By the way, about one half of the marriages in the U.S. end in divorce. Instead of saying, "that could never happen to me," consider understanding what I am trying to say. This will increase your chances of marrying your last partner first.

Now let's look at some tips for dating.

TIPS FOR DATING

- Dating is a process to learn about yourself and to eventually choose the best partner with whom to create a lasting relationship.

- Romantic love is not predictive of lasting love, so go slowly when you have a "crush" on someone.

- Take a small risk to get things started; smile or say hi first.

- To play the dating game, pretend you have a hand of cards. Each of these cards represents a fact about yourself. Show only one card at a time. If it is matched with one from the other person, share another of yours. It is a common mistake to either show your whole hand of cards or none at all.

- Learn to "chit chat." Effective small talk allows you to find out whether or not the other person has potential for you.

- When you are a young teen, go out with a group of friends. The one-on-one relating is best if you wait until high school.

- It is easy to get tricked by your feelings and emotions, so know you will make mistakes and sometimes look foolish. Remember to learn from all your choices and experiences.

- Look deeper than the physical side of the relationship. Spend time being a "detective" to find out the other person's real personality. The more you find out about a person before going with them the less surprised you'll be further down the road.

- Observe the family of the person you are dating. Does this person relate well to their mother? father? siblings? What do you notice that looks or feels "off"?

- Communicate—talk and listen—to each other. Go behind the words to the feelings and deeper meanings of conversations. Express yourself!

- Feelings of insecurity, jealousy, or possessiveness are red flags. They almost always mean there are problems that may mean you need to go back through this book and relearn what loving yourself is all about.

- Observe your own parents' and grandparents' relationships. Their patterns were passed on to you without even trying. Understand this before entering a permanent relationship.

REMEMBER NOT TO TAKE THE DATING GAME TOO SERIOUSLY!

QUESTIONS ABOUT
PEER PRESSURE
FOR JOURNAL WRITING
OR GROUP DISCUSSION

1. Why are many teens unhappy if they do not have a boy or girlfriend?

2. Have you ever ignored your code of values when you were dating someone? Explain why this happens with some people? What advice do you have to help people stick to and honor their code of values?

3. What does peer pressure mean to you? Is it always negative?

4. Why does wearing brand name clothing, that is popular with friends, give a false sense of security and self-esteem?

5. Why do you think some teens use alcohol and drugs before going to a party? What would be a better way to handle this?

6. At what age do you think negative peer pressure is the strongest? For you personally, what has been the most difficult situation you have been pressured about doing?

7. What are the risks in saying "no" to pressure from friends that goes against your values? Why do you think some teens say "yes" when they really want to say "no"?

8. What draws teens to certain people who make decisions for the group? What characteristics does the leader have? Have you ever been the leader in your peer group? Why?

9. Do you think resisting peer pressure increases or decreases with age? How has it been in your life so far?

10. If you were to project yourself into the future, how do you see yourself dealing with negative peer pressure in two years? What will you be able to do then that you are not able to do now? Answer the same questions for five years in the future.

11. Do you think older teens out of high school and adults feel pressure from peers? Give examples.

12. Are there any positive benefits to peer pressure? What needs are met by being included in a group?

13. Have you ever had a friend that your parents did not like. Write about the situation from your point of view. Your parents' point of view. Do you listen to your parents' opinions? Why? Have you ever made a change of friendship because of pressure from your parents?

14. Does the pull between parental pressure and peer pressure cause confusion and stress for you at times? How? Give an example.

15. What have you learned so far about doing what is right for you versus going along with the crowd? Do you voice your opinion? Why?

16. List eight to ten values that your mother has. Your father has. Are your values similar to your mother's values? Father's? Other family member's? Friend's family values? Explain and give examples.

17. Are you strong enough within yourself to be with friends who make wrong choices and still not participate? Why do you think this is so? If you are not strong enough to resist what do you think would be wise for you to think about?

18. If there were no pressure from school, friends, parents...what is the most exciting, creative, and challenging things you would be doing? If money, time, and education were set aside what would you be doing for a job or career as an adult? Describe what your relationships would look like? Do you think it is possible to have this good future? Why?

FINAL AFFIRMATION:

I love and support myself

with wise choices as

I experience my life

and grow into my

Full Potential Self.

NOTES

Suzanne inspires people to build awareness and improve their lives through counseling, telephone consultations, writing, workshops, and public speaking. She is a natural teacher, encourages self-discovery, and facilitates others in becoming their own authority. Empowering clients to heal their own life, to build a solid foundation of self-esteem, and to live with meaning and purpose are top  priorities in her work. In the state of Texas Suzanne is a Licensed Marriage and Family Therapist and a Licensed Professional Counselor.

Originally trained as an art teacher, Suzanne later earned her masters degree in education, specializing in counseling psychology. Her experience includes teaching children, adolescents, adults, and college students. In 1981 she started a private counseling practice and began teaching self-esteem workshops for adults. Her first book, published in 1987, initiated her writing career. See her many works on her website.

The mission statement of Innerworks is, "To empower people to love and accept themselves, to heal pain from the past, to know their purpose, and to reach their potential individually and collectively."

Suzanne is married, has three grown daughters, is a grandmother, and currently lives in Castle Rock, Colorado. She enjoys traveling, hiking in nature, reading, watercolor painting, creating original stained glass pieces, and spending time with her family and friends.

Contact Suzanne on her website to receive her free on-line, self-help newsletter, to order books, or for personal telephone consultations.

Innerworks Counseling & Publishing
www.InnerworksPublishing.com
167 Glengarry Place
Castle Rock, CO 80108

Self-Help Books by Suzanne E. Harrill

Adults
Enlightening Cinderella
Beyond the Prince Charming Fantasy........................ $12.95
A Simple Self-Esteem Guide (Booklet)........................ 3.00
Empowering You to Love Yourself (e-book only)............ 10.00
Inner Fitness for Creating a Better You: Six Lessons for
Building Greater Awareness, High Self-Esteem, Good
Relationships, and Spiritual Meaning (worksheets to copy).... 24.95
* E-books $10 each at www.InnerworksPublishing.com

Forthcoming Books
Becoming the Person You Always Wanted to Marry:
Relationship as a Path to Wholeness
Seed Thoughts for Loving Yourself:
A Daily Affirmation Book

Adolescents
Empowering Teens To Build Self-Esteem........................ 16.95
Exploring * Connecting * Emerging
6wk. Adolescent Self-Esteem Curriculum w/worksheets... 89.00

For Children
I Am a STAR, My Building High Self-Esteem Book.......... 12.95
I Am a STAR: Self-Esteem Affirmation Cards................ 14.95

Shipping in USA: $4.05 first item, $1.00 each additional item

**Order on-line with credit card www.InnerworksPublishing.com
or send check/money order made out to Suzanne Harrill to:**

Innerworks Publishing
167 Glengarry Pl.
Castle Rock, CO 80108

Sign up for free on-line newsletter to spark the inner journey!

www.InnerworksPublishing.com

LaVergne, TN USA
07 December 2010
207621LV00003B/4/P

9 781883 648046